It's Not JUNK It's RESOURCES!

by Tina Houser

©2007 by Warner Press Inc Anderson, IN 46018

www.warnerpress.org

All rights reserved

ISBN: 978-1-59317-214-5

Editor: Karen Rhodes

Photography: Michael Meadows

Design & Illustrations: Curt Corzine/Christian Elden/Kevin Spear

Printed in USA

Warner Press Kids™
educate • nurture • inspire
www.warnerpress.org

31795017673

Table of Contents

Thank You!

Heather Ferren
Cierra Ferren
Colton Ferren
Heidi Johnson
Hannah Johnson

Sarah Johnson
Seth Johnson
Stacy Lawson
Casey Lawson
Kara Lawson

Rachel Lawson
Cheryl Evans
and of course, tina!

Explanation of icons

 = indoor games

 = outoor games

The other icons represent the main object used in the project.

It's not Junk... It's Resources!

When I first accepted the position as Minister of Children at First Church of God in Kokomo, my small office also served as the Sunday school office, and where all resources for children's ministry were housed.

Most often it was a collage—piles of newspaper, toilet rolls, hula hoops, Frisbees—all kinds of miscellaneous objects people had brought to me, thinking I might find some unique way of using them. As the kick-off date for a big project neared, such as Bible school, there was only a small walking path from the door to my chair.

Calvin had just joined our church's staff as youth pastor and this was his first exposure to children's ministry. One day several people were standing in the hallway and I heard Calvin refer to the contents of my office as "Tina's junk." My eyebrows raised and I gave him "the look."

During the next few weeks he watched teachers come and go out of my office, gathering some of the strange items I kept there. The next time I heard him refer to my office he called it "Tina's stuff."

"Well," I thought to myself, "at least it's not junk anymore." Then Calvin experienced a full-blown week of Bible school where almost everything that was in my office and covering the floor was brought out. Each item was used to reach kids, who had come from all over our city, with the message that God loves them and so do we. The next time Calvin referred to my office, he called it "Tina's resources" and then threw me an understanding grin.

tina!

It's Time to Think Creatively!

This book is about seeing things in a different light. Creativity is changing the context of something… finding a new way to use an object rather than for its intended use. Find an interesting object in your kitchen or garage and create a learning tool from it. Use these exercises to stir the fires of creativity within you as you look at everyday objects in a new light.

Exercise 1

Look at one of the following objects and come up with five things you could do with it, other than its normal function:

Flyswatter

Large Styrofoam™ cup

Potato chip can

Potato masher

Styrofoam™ burger box

_____

_____

_____

_____

_____

_____

_____

_____

_____

Exercise 2

Choose a color. With a partner, name as many things that are that color as you can in two minutes.

_____

_____

_____

_____

_____

_____

_____

_____

_____

_____

_____

_____

Exercise 3

Cut a 1-inch square out of a piece of cardstock. Ask someone to choose a picture from a magazine like *National Geographic* and lay the cardstock over the picture so you see only one inch of the picture. Make up several realities of what the entire picture could be, based on the one inch that can be seen.

_____

_____

_____

_____

_____

_____

_____

_____

_____

Exercise 4

Play the Props Game with a group of people. Place a common object or a pair of objects in the center of the room. Whenever someone thinks of something they could imitate using that object they get up and act it out. Try using a grass skirt, two reflectors on metal sticks, and a wrapping paper roller that has been unwound.

_____

_____

_____

_____

_____

_____

_____

_____

_____

_____

And, if you're saying to yourself right now that you're just not a creative person, let me remind you of one mind-boggling truth. God is the Great Creator. In Genesis 1:27, one of the very first things we learn about man when God created him was that God created people in His own image. God patterned them after Himself. If God has patterned us after Him, and He is the Creator, the master of creativity, then we have within us the ability to be creative. Explore your creativity and give it a chance to blossom. And have fun!

Human Chain
CHAIN GANG

This activity can be used with any story that has at least 5 tangible items that can be collected. Each team will need a similar set of items. Think of the story of the Prodigal Son, or as I like to call it, the story of the "Loving Father." Five objects related to this story that could be used are: a stuffed pig, a large ring, a sandal, a party hat, fake money (Luke 15:11-32).

Resource Preparation & Fun #1:

- Form two teams. Because boys don't usually like to hold hands with girls (and vice versa), this game is probably played easier with teams of boys and girls, if there are equal numbers of each.
- Each team will form a chain by holding hands, with the 5 items at one end of the chain.
- At the signal, the end person on each chain will pick up one of the items. (The teams do not have to go in the same order. Any item they want to pick up is fine.)
- Never in the game can the players break loose from the person(s) they have hold of. (Kids can pass items with their hands, just moving them together, but not breaking loose, or pass items between their chins and shoulders, even with their feet! Let them be creative.)
- The first player passes the item to the person they are holding hands with and tells them something about the item, relating it to the story. (If the party hat was picked up, the player may say, "The son spent his money having parties with his friends.")
- The second player would then pass the item to the next player, telling something about the item. It doesn't have to be something new; they can repeat what has already been said.

- Remind the kids "Don't break the chain!"
- When the item reaches the last person, the next item can start down the chain.
- The object is to get all five objects to the other end of the chain.

Resource #2 for Palm Sunday:

- The children will pass palm branches down their chain.
- When the last player gets a palm branch, he or she holds on to it.
- The next branch passed will stop at the child who is second from the end, and so on, until all the children have a palm branch.
- Without breaking the human chain, wave the branches in the air together and say, "Hosanna! Hosanna!"

Suggested Stories:

- Zacchaeus: bag of coins, leaf, branch, loaf of bread, an invitation
- The Boy Who Shared His Lunch: brown lunch sack, a dinner roll, plastic fish, basket, a male doll to represent the boy
- Jesus Was Born: star, baby blanket, stuffed sheep, halo (ring of gold tinsel), jeweled box
- The Twelve Spies: plastic bottle of honey, a small carton of milk, bunch of grapes, plastic grasshopper, spy glass
- Joseph in Prison: silver cup, bunch of grapes, basket, bread, bird

Acoustical Tile
PORTABLE BULLETIN BOARD/STORY BOARDS

"Junk" Needed for Resource #1

Acoustical ceiling tile

Used plastic tablecloth

Bulletin board border

Duct tape

Hot Glue gun

Resource #1

Cover an acoustical ceiling tile with a bright-colored plastic tablecloth. Use a hot glue gun to attach the tablecloth to the back of the tile. Then finish the edges with bulletin board border to make a portable bulletin board.

Resource #2

Cover an acoustical ceiling tile with black flannel. Copy story figures (silhouettes) onto neon paper and cut them out. Attach a small piece of Velcro™ to the back of each piece. Place a black light in front of the black covered tile in a completely dark room. When the neon figures are placed on the board they will glow in the dark.

"Junk" Needed for Resource #2

Acoustical ceiling tile

Blacklight

Black flannel

Neon paper

Velcro™

"Junk" Needed for Resource #3

Acoustical ceiling tile

Light blue flannel

Resource #3

Cover the tiles with light blue flannel for a traditional flannelgraph board. Make enough for each child to have his or her own.

A Sabbath Prescription
BABY FOOD JARS

"Junk" Needed:
Baby food jars
Mailing labels
Markers
Prescription bottle

Hold up the prescription bottle.

Ask:

- What do you find in a bottle like this?
- Why do you take the medicine that the doctor has prescribed?
- Did you know that God has given us a prescription that will help keep us healthy: physically, mentally, emotionally, and spiritually?
- Do you remember the story of creation where God created different things on six days?

Review what God created each day:

Day 1: God divided the dark and the light.

Day 2: God separated space and water.

Day 3: He created the land, the seas, and the plants.

Day 4: God created the sun, moon, and stars.

Day 5: God created the fish and the birds.

Day 6: God created animals, man and woman.

Ask:

- What did God do on the seventh day?
- Later in the Bible, when God gave the 10 Commandments, He included a commandment that said, "Keep the Sabbath day holy."
- What does holy mean? (separate, set apart)
- What are we supposed to do on the Sabbath day? (focus on worshiping God, rest)
- How do you act when you're tired? (cranky, get angry easily, don't want to do anything) When we don't rest, our bodies get worn out and we get sick more easily. When we have too much to do then we don't have time to rest. We also don't have time to concentrate on God, so we're pushing Him out of our lives. We need to make time to rest and focus on God. A good day of rest and worship will get you ready to tackle a brand new week.

Continued on next page

A Sabbath Prescription
CONTINUED

Resource Preparation & Fun:

- Give each child a baby food jar and a mailing label.
- Write "Sabbath Prescription" on the label and use some colorful markers to decorate the label.
- Each child will write on small slips of paper some ways he or she could personally keep the Sabbath day holy.
- Roll these up and place them in the jar.

Here are some suggestions to get the thoughts going in the right direction. Write these ideas on the board for kids to see.

- Go for a long walk and thank God for the things I hear.
- Call a grandparent who lives far away.
- Curl up with my dog and take a nap.
- Go to breakfast with a friend and then attend church together.
- Paint what is outside my window.

Say:

Take your Sabbath Prescription home to remind you that there is a day of rest coming. On the Sabbath, pull out one of the slips of paper and use that way to connect with God and to rest your body and mind.

Balloon Scramble
VERSE MEMORIZATION OR STORY HELPER

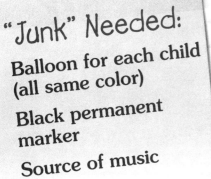

"Junk" Needed:

Balloon for each child (all same color)

Black permanent marker

Source of music

Resource Fun #1 -

Use this when each child is trying to memorize a different scripture.

- Write each scripture address (reference) on a balloon. Make sure the balloons are all the same color.
- At the signal the kids will bat the balloons around the room while the music plays.
- It doesn't matter which balloon they hit; they can hit any balloon that comes near.
- When the music stops, the kids will scramble to find the balloon that has the scripture address (reference) on it that they are trying to memorize.

Resource Fun #2 –

Use this for reinforcing a Bible story.

- Write a brief description of each scene in the Bible story on a balloon.
- Play the music and bat around the balloons.
- When the music stops the children grab the balloon that is closest to them.
- The kids will put the story together in sequential order as they share what is on each of their balloons.

Carrying a Friend
FOUR FRIENDS AND A BALLOON

"Junk" Needed:

Balloon

Black permanent marker

2 strips of old sheeting (12" wide)

As you study the story of the four men who let their friend down through the roof in order to bring him to Jesus, add a physical activity to reinforce the story using the "junk" listed above.

The Main Thing – Luke 5:18-26

The man in this story had been sick for a long time, but he had some good friends who cared about him very much. The four friends carried the man carefully on his mat to Jesus. We don't know how far the friends carried the man, but it couldn't have been easy for them. They had to carry him up on top of the house and then lower him through the hole they had made in the roof.

Say:

Carry the balloon as carefully as the friend would have carried the man.

Resource Preparation & Fun:

- Blow up a balloon and draw a face on it with a black permanent marker to represent the man who needed to be healed.

- Rip two strips of old sheeting lengthwise from the sheet, about twelve inches wide. Lay the two strips of sheeting across one another in an "X" and place the balloon where the strips intersect.

- Four children will play at a time. Each one picks up the end of one of the strips.

- Determine a place that will represent the house where Jesus was.

- The object is for the four children to carry the balloon to the designated place without letting the balloon fall off the sheet.

Joseph Prepares for the Famine

BALLOONS O'PLENTY

"Junk" Needed:

Large empty closet

Lots of balloons

The Main Thing - Genesis 40—42

When Joseph was able to tell the Pharaoh what his dream meant, Pharaoh trusted Joseph with a very important job. If the famine was going to happen in seven years, then the country needed to be prepared. Joseph's job was to make sure enough food was stored for the years when the food would not grow.

Resource Preparation & Fun:

- Blow up a large supply of balloons. The kids can help do this, but if you want to maximize the use of your time, have them ready beforehand.

- Place the balloons as far away from an empty closet as possible.

Say:

- *Let's pretend all these balloons are the extra crops that everyone in Egypt had and the closet is the storehouse where Joseph was storing the food.*

- *At my signal try to get all the balloons into the storehouse. You can't hold onto the balloons, but you can bat them with your hands.*

- Once a balloon has made it into the closet, each player can go back and move another balloon into the storehouse. (All players grab 1 balloon at a time, put it in the closet, then go get another balloon.)

Squirt the Halo
BALLOON ANGELS

"Junk" Needed:
Duct tape
Large balloon
Permanent black marker
Plastic drop cloth
Shaving cream
Squirt gun

Resource Preparation & Fun:

Enjoy this activity anytime an angel appears in the story you are studying. It's an **outside** activity, but if you must bring it indoors, use an abundant supply of drop cloths.

- Each child will blow up his or her balloon and tie it off.
- Then, have them draw an angel face on their balloon, but **don't** put a halo on it.
- Duct tape two balloons to the edge of a table, several feet apart.
- If indoors, lay a drop cloth underneath and cover the back wall.
- The leader should make a halo on each of the angel balloons with shaving cream.
- Position two players whose balloons are taped to the table, behind the designated line.
- At the signal they will squirt the balloons using squirt guns and try to remove the shaving cream halos.

Ask:

Why was the angel important in this story?

Why did God send an angel in this story?

How do you think you would react if an angel appeared to you?

Goal Roll
GYM BALL SOCCER

Resource Fun:

- Divide the kids into two equal teams. Designate the teams by the color ball you give them.
- Seat the kids cross-legged and scattered all over a large room.
- At each end of the room, make a rectangle (goal) on the floor about 2' x 3' using masking tape. (If you have colored masking tape, coordinate the goals with the color of the team.)
- Tell the teams which goal belongs to their team.
- To start the game, place both balls in the center of the room.

Say:

- The object of the game is to be the first team to get your ball to pass through your goal area.
- All players will be moving your ball toward your goal, while at the same time trying to keep the other team's ball from getting to their goal.
- The ball can be touched only with your hands and it must stay on the ground and roll at all times.
- When a ball passes through its goal area, a point is scored.
- We will play until one team makes three points.
- Remember to keep your eyes on the goal and the opponent's balls!

Give the children one of these scriptures to look up:

Hebrews 12:1-2

1 Timothy 6:11-12

2 Timothy 4:7

1 Corinthians 9:24

After the verses have been read aloud, ask these questions:

- As Christians, who are we to keep focused on at all times?
- How can focusing on Jesus strengthen our faith?
- What might happen if we don't keep our eyes and hearts on following Jesus?

Say:

It's so important to keep our focus on Jesus every day, just like it was important to focus on our ball in order to get it to the goal. The other team's ball kept distracting us.

- What kinds of things distract you from being the person God wants you to be?
- Many things, such as lies, bad choices, and unkind thoughts, try to steer us away from following Jesus.
- But, when we keep our hearts and minds focused on Him and doing what He would do, we're all winners!

Temptation Stations
OBSTACLE COURSE

"Junk" Needed:

4" x 4" x 8' beam

2 concrete blocks

Bucket

Duct tape

Inflatable clown (or other weighted inflatable object)

Small pieces of foam or Styrofoam™ peanuts

Small one-step stepstool

The Main Thing – Luke 4:1-13

Before beginning His ministry, Jesus went into the desert for 40 days to prepare for the mission that was in front of Him. After 40 days, Satan came to Jesus who was tired and hungry from not eating the entire time. Satan tried to tempt Jesus to follow him rather than stay true to God (Matthew 4:1-11, Luke 4:1-13). What did Jesus do each time Satan tempted him?

Resource Preparation & Fun:

Each child will go through the temptation stations to represent the temptations of Christ. The stations should be about 15 feet from one another.

- At station one there will be a bucket of foam pieces or Styrofoam™ peanuts (bread) and some pretend rocks (wadded up duct tape).
- At station two there will be the beam that is lifted off the ground by a concrete block at each end.
- Station three is where the inflatable weighted object will be.
- Then, place a stepstool at station four.
- The kids will take turns going through the stations.
- One child should complete all four stations before the next child begins.
- At the first station they will search through the bucket to find a duct tape rock among the foam pieces and lay the rock on the ground next to the bucket. This represents the fact that although Satan tempted Jesus, who had been without food for 40 days, to turn the rocks into bread, Jesus would not do it.

- At the next station, children will walk from one end of the balance beam to the other. When they exit the beam, they yell out, "Jesus would not jump off!" This represents that Jesus would not jump from the roof of the temple as Satan tempted Him to do.
- At the third station, they will punch the inflatable weighted object and say, "Get away from me, Satan!" Finally, they will jump up on the stepstool and raise their hands up over their head in triumph, yelling, "Jesus won over evil!"

It is very important that the children say the phrases that go along with each station. These phrases bring home the point of the exercise.

Several courses can be set up to run at the same time if you have a large number of children. You could even have groups competing against each other.

Crossing the River

JUMPING RACE

Use this activity to go along with stories where people were crossing a river or sea, such as Crossing the Jordan River or Crossing of the Red Sea.

Resource Preparation & Fun:

- Lay two, 2" x 4" boards of equal length parallel to one another.

- The children will jump over the boards.

- Move the boards so there is a 6" space between them and then the children will jump over them again.

- The river is wider than that so move the boards a little further apart.

- The river is wider than that!

- After each time the children jump over the boards, move them a little further apart and remind them that the river is wider than that.

- Once a child cannot make the jump, he or she steps out and watches until the boards are too far for everyone.

Royal Toss
BEANBAG FOR A CROWN

"Junk" Needed:

12 cardboard crowns from a fast food restaurant

Beanbags

Masking tape

Resource Preparation:

Many stories in the Bible include a person of royalty. All of these are good places to add this game for a fun way of reviewing. If you do not have a fast food restaurant that has the cardboard crowns for kids, then make some out of poster board.

Resource Preparation & Fun:

- Create 12 questions about the story and write these on scraps of paper.

- Place the crowns in a group with one of the questions inside each crown.

- Leave about 8" of space between the crowns.

- Mark a stand-behind line on the floor with a piece of masking tape.

- The kids will take turns standing behind the masking tape and tossing a beanbag at the crowns.

- If the beanbag goes inside one of the crowns completely, then the player will retrieve the question that is inside the crown.

- If the child is a reader, he or she may want to read the question; otherwise, the leader will read the question about the story.

- If the question is answered correctly, the child may remove the crown from play.

Hit the Breastplate
BEANBAG THROW

"Junk" Needed:
Beanbags
Piece of cardboard

Although a piece of cardboard isn't much protection, it can be used in this activity to teach about the armor of God, which definitely provides protection.

Resource Preparation:

- Cut out a piece of cardboard to look like a breastplate, then, hang it on the wall.
- Prepare a set of situation cards where the child will have to make a choice about whether to do right or wrong.

Say:

- One piece of the armor of God is the breastplate of righteousness. Do you know what righteousness is?
- The answer is right there in the beginning of that big word. It's doing what's right in the sight of God.
- The breastplate is the piece that covers the chest, protecting the heart.
- When we choose to do right in all situations, we protect our heart from Satan taking control of it.

Resource Fun:

- Determine a stand-behind line about eight feet from the breastplate that is hanging on the wall.
- Each child will get three tries to hit the breastplate with a beanbag.
- If he or she is successful, draw one of the cards that have been prepared and read it. The child should respond with the righteous (right) thing to do in that situation.

Bottle Bowling

SURPRISE QUESTIONS

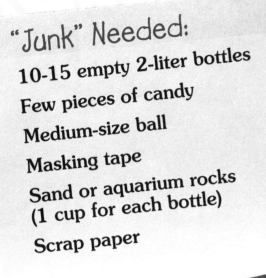

"Junk" Needed:

10-15 empty 2-liter bottles

Few pieces of candy

Medium-size ball

Masking tape

Sand or aquarium rocks
(1 cup for each bottle)

Scrap paper

This is an easy-to-prepare generic game that can be used with just about any lesson.

Resource Preparation & Fun:

- Prepare 10-15 empty 2-liter bottles by placing one cup of sand or aquarium rocks in each one.
- Secure the cap.
- The weight of the sand will keep the bottles from falling over too easily
  (or the wind from blowing them away if playing outside).
- Write a question about the story on a scrap piece of paper and tape it on the outside of the bottle.
- If there are more bottles than questions, then put "Surprise!" on the extras.
- Mark a stand-behind line with masking tape about 20 feet from the bottles.
- Place the bottles in a line about a foot apart, so they won't easily knock one another over.
- The children will take turns rolling the ball from behind the line.
- If a bottle is knocked over, then that child will try to answer the question on the side of it.
- If "Surprise!" is written on the bottle, then the child receives a
  piece of candy and has a pass on the question.
- Continue playing until all the bottles have been knocked over.

Box of Faith

SHIELD OF FAITH RACE

"Junk" Needed:
2 large boxes

Say:

The Bible tells us to use every piece of the armor of God. Faith is to be our shield. Faith is believing in something, even when we can't see it. We can't see God, but we believe in Him.

Resource Fun:

- Position two large boxes at the start line.
- Show the children where the finish line is.
- Choose a child to get under each of the boxes.
- Then, choose another child to be the guide for each box to tell those underneath where to move.
- At the signal, both of the kids under the boxes will head for the finish line, keeping the box down over them.
- The children outside the box will try to tell them where to go.
- The object is to get the box across the finish line without lifting up the box to look.

Say:

You couldn't see the person who was telling you how to get to the finish line, but you believed she was there. You had faith in her to get you where you wanted to go. God's Word, the Bible, guides us and tells us how to live so we can be winners in the race of life. We need to listen to what it tells us, even though we can't see God physically.

Hole in One
BROOM GOLF

"Junk" Needed:

2 buckets

Broom for each child

Golf ball for each child

Masking tape

Resource Preparation & Fun #1:

- Create questions for the Bible lesson of your choosing that can be answered "Yes" or "No." (Or, situational questions that can be answered "Right" or "Wrong.")
- Label the buckets "Yes" and "No" (or "Right" and "Wrong") and lay them on their sides.
- Several children can play at once, so give each player a broom and a golf ball.
- With a small piece of masking tape, mark a place for each child to place his or her golf ball.
- Read one of the questions. The players hurry and use their brooms to sweep their golf balls into the correct bucket ("Yes" or "No").
- The golf ball does not have to stay in the bucket, but it must go all the way in.
- Place the golf balls back on the masking tape lines and go for the next question.

Resource Fun #2

- Place one bucket on its side.
- Ask a question
- The children who know the answer race to see who can get their golf ball into the bucket first.
- Whoever gets their ball in first gets to answer the question.

A Bucket Full of Servanthood
SHOWING LOVE WITH BEANBAGS

"Junk" Needed:
5 buckets
4 beanbags
Masking tape

The Main Thing – 1 John 4:7-8

They will know we are Christians by our love. Kids are very capable of demonstrating God's love to people around them and to people they will never come in direct contact with.

Before proceeding with this game, discuss ways the children can be involved personally in touching the lives of others in their families, at their school, in their church, in their community, and throughout the world. Try to be very practical with the ideas so the kids feel they could actually accomplish them.

Resource Preparation & Fun:

* Label the buckets: **family, school, church, community,** and **world**.
* Set the buckets in a line, one behind the other.
* Determine a stand-behind line about five feet away from the first bucket.
* The first player will try to toss a beanbag into the first bucket.
* If he is successful, he names a way to show love to the group on the bucket's label.
* Then, he tosses again, trying to get the beanbag into the second bucket.
* If successful, he names a way to show love to that group.
* Continue until he no longer makes a good toss (throw 'til you miss!).
* After each successful player, mix the order of the buckets.

Hauling Bricks
NEHEMIAH'S WALL

"Junk" Needed:
Bricks
Wheelbarrow
Work gloves

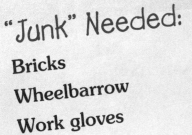

Do you have leftover bricks from a building project and don't know what to do with them besides stack them against the back of the house? Prepare a set of questions about Nehemiah rebuilding the wall of Jerusalem. Write these on index cards and tape each one to a brick. Place the bricks in a pile about 30 feet away.

The Main Thing - Nehemiah 2:19—6:19

Say:

The wall surrounding Jerusalem was in shambles, and God put the burden on Nehemiah's heart to rebuild it. But, he didn't do it by himself. Each person worked diligently at the job they were assigned to do. Although there were obstacles and threats along the way, Nehemiah led the people to complete the wall. Do you think the people ever doubted that the wall could be rebuilt? Why do you think they were able to complete it?

Resource Fun:

- The kids will take turns putting on a pair of work gloves and pushing the wheelbarrow down to the pile of bricks.

- Each child will grab a brick, place it in the wheelbarrow, and return to the starting line.

- Each player is to hold onto the brick they have retrieved.

- Once all the bricks have been returned, the children will take turns reading the question on their brick and responding to it.

- Then, stack the bricks to make a small wall.

This can also be played with a toy wheelbarrow and bricks made of milk cartons.

The Winds Came
THE WISE AND FOOLISH MAN

"Junk" Needed:

3 cardboard toilet tissue rollers

Construction paper

The Main Thing - Matthew 7:24-26

Reinforce the story of the wise man and the foolish man with this activity.

Say:

Jesus told about two different kinds of men—a wise man and a foolish man. He told about how each man built a house.

- What happened that threatened the houses? (terrible rains, floodwaters, high winds)
- What happened to the wise man's house when the rains and the wind came?
- Why did it stand?
- What happened to the foolish man's house when the rains and the wind came?
- Why did it fall?

Resource Preparation & Fun:

- Make 3 simple house shapes out of construction paper.
- Cut them out and tape each to a toilet tissue roller.
- Place the houses at the edge of a table.
- Also, determine a stand-behind line with masking tape or rope, 3-4 feet from the table.

Say:

We're going to see if our winds can blow down the foolish man's house.

- Choose three children to play at a time.
- Have each child stand at the indicated line in front of one of the houses.
- At your signal, they will try to blow hard enough to make their house fall over.
- The main rule is that they cannot bend in toward their house when blowing.
- When one of the houses falls over, then three new players are chosen.

Upside Down Ring Toss

CARNIVAL GAME

Resource Preparation & Fun:

This carnival type game is fun to add to any lesson. Do you have a chair that is not quite stable enough for a kid to sit in safely? Don't throw it out; make it into a upside down ring toss.

- Turn the chair upside down and each leg becomes a peg for a ring toss.
- Homemade toss rings can be made by cutting the center from some plastic margarine or whipped topping lids.
- Determine a stand-behind line by putting down a piece of masking tape.

When a child is successful at getting a ring to go over a leg of the chair...

- Ask him a question about the story
- Ask her to respond to a situation, or
- Ask them to recite the memory verse they have been working on. The physical activity takes the intensity out of learning.
- Have fun!

"Junk" Needed:

An old chair

Masking tape

Plastic lids (from margarine or whipped topping)

Rubber Band Round-Up
DIGGING FOR A STORY

Resource Preparation & Fun:

- Prepare a set of questions about the story that is being taught.
- Fill a large plastic or galvanized tub with play sand.
- Then mix a large supply of colored rubber bands into the sand thoroughly.
- Form two teams. Give each team one chopstick.
- At your signal one player from each team will dig in the sand with his or her chopstick, trying to find the rubber bands.
- At no time can players put their hands in the sand or touch a rubber band.
- Play stops when one player gets three rubber bands on his or her chopstick.
- Ask the player with the three rubber bands a question about the story.
- If he or she answers correctly, the player puts the rubber bands around his or her wrist.
- If the player answers incorrectly, the other player gets to keep whatever rubber bands he or she was able to get on his or her chopstick.
- If other children are waiting to play, start the next round with new players to give everyone an opportunity to play.

"Junk" Needed:

Ballpoint pen

Bucket

Supply of spring clothespins

Resource Preparation & Fun:

There's not much use for clothespins anymore, but they can be put to good use in this activity that helps in scripture memorization (for readers).

- For each child, prepare a set of clothespins by writing one word of each scripture memory verse on a clothespin.
- Use a ballpoint pen, and not a marker, because the ink from a marker will bleed into the wood.
- Older children will be able to prepare their own set of clothespins.
- The verses can all be the same scripture, or a mixture of scriptures can be used at the same time.
- Throw all the clothespins into a bucket, mixing the sets thoroughly.
- Toss the clothespins out on the floor.
- The kids will retrieve clothespins that have words from their verse until they have the entire verse retrieved.
- Each time they pick up a clothespin, they attach it to their clothes.
- When all have the verse completed and are covered in clothespins, say the verse together.
- As each word is said have the kids pull that word off of their clothing.

A Walk to Emmaus
STILTS IN A CAN

Interject this activity into a lesson on the story of the Road to Emmaus (Luke 24:13-32). Let your imagination go and figure out other uses for these fun makeshift stilts.

"Junk" Needed:
5-foot piece of clothesline rope
Drill
Duct tape
Empty coffee cans

Resource Preparation & Fun:

- Prepare two coffee cans for each child.
- Turn the can upside down and drill a ½" hole in each side of the can close to the top (which is really the bottom).
- Seal the edges of the holes by covering them with duct tape.
- Thread one end of a piece of clothesline rope into one hole (from the outside) and tie a knot at the end (on the inside of the can).
- Do the same for the other end of the rope in the hole on the other side of the can.
- Make a sign that says "Jerusalem", a sign that says "Emmaus", and seven-mile markers, labeled 1-7.
- Position the nine signs about 5 feet apart: Jerusalem, 7 miles, 1, 2, 3, 4, 5, 6, 7, Emmaus.
- The kids will stand on the coffee cans and hold onto the rope loop.
- They will begin in Jerusalem and walk to the mile one marker using their coffee can stilts.
- When they get to the first marker they should yell "One mile!"
- Then they will continue walking on the stilts to the two-mile marker where they should yell, "Two miles!"
- The kids will continue their "journey" until they get to Emmaus where they say, "It's Jesus!" and then run all the way back to Jerusalem without stopping.
- Several children can go on their walk together or they can be sent one at a time.

Ask:

- Why were the men going to Emmaus from Jerusalem?
- What did the men realize when they got to Emmaus?
- Why did they come back so quickly after traveling seven miles?

Going on a Journey
HEADS OR TAILS QUEST

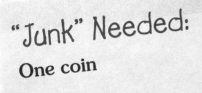

"Junk" Needed:

One coin

The Main Thing

Use this activity with any story where God is leading the people on a journey or to find something (God leading the Israelites through the desert, Eliezer being sent for a wife for Isaac, Joshua leading the Israelites into the Promised Land, Paul's journeys, the disciples going after the donkey for Jesus to ride into Jerusalem).

- How did they know where to go?
- Was there something they should look for along the way?

Resource Fun:

- Take the children on a journey.
- The way to decide where they will go is by a flip of a coin.
- Stand at the classroom door and flip the coin.
- If it is "heads," then turn right.
- If it is "tails," then turn left.
- Each time the children come to where hallways cross or there's a dead end, toss the coin to decide which way to go.

Ask:

- Is this the way God led the people in today's story?
- How did God lead them?
- Did they find what they were looking for?

Pennies for Hunger Relay

A 22¢ MEAL

"Junk" Needed:

Place setting for each team (plate, fork, spoon, knife, cup, napkin)

22 pennies in a cup for each team

Have you ever seen people give back their penny when receiving change or put it in a little receptacle by the cash register? Or, maybe a penny was laying in a puddle, but no one bothered to pick it up? That's because people consider a penny as worthless…it's junk in the eyes of many! Use this activity to show children pennies that others might think aren't worth picking up can have a huge impact on those who are hungry.

Ask:

- How much does a Happy Meal™ cost?
- How much is an order of French fries at your favorite restaurant?
- There are organizations that concentrate on feeding the hungry children in places where people are starving.
- The people in those organizations tell us that 22 cents is all it costs for them to provide a meal for a hungry child.
- That doesn't seem like very much.
- How many meals could be provided with the money spent on one Happy Meal™?

Resource Preparation:

- Divide the players into two teams. (The point can be made with just one team if you have a small number of kids, and the number of teams can be expanded for a large group.)
- At the far end of a large room, set up a place setting for each team to represent a meal.
- Each team will have a cup with 22 pennies in it.
- The object of both of these variations to the game is to get the 22 pennies on the plate, which represents feeding a hungry child.

Resource Fun #1:

- Spread out the players on each team so they stretch from the starting point where the cup of pennies is, to the place setting.
- It does not matter the distance between the players.
- At the signal, each team will take one penny from the cup and pass it from player to player until it gets to the plate.
- When the last player places the penny on the plate, he or she will yell "More!" and the next penny can be passed through the players.
- The game is over when the team gets all 22 pennies to their plate.

Say:

- There are now enough pennies on this plate to buy a meal for a hungry child.
- How did the pennies get here?
- They were passed from one person to the next.
- When we give money to feed a hungry child, we don't just buy the food and hand it to them. The money goes through other people's hands.
- We may send our money to World Vision™, an organization that feeds children around the world.
- They purchase food and send it on a plane to a country in Africa. Someone meets the plane and takes the food to a village.
- Those people give the food to someone who works with the villagers, and that person makes sure the children are fed.
- The money we give goes through several sets of hands before it actually feeds someone. When we give, we should remember to pray for all those hands that are making sure the children are fed.

Resource Fun #2:

- At the signal one child from each team will take a penny to the place setting and deposit it on the plate.
- He or she will return to the team and tag the next player, who will carry the next penny to the plate.
- This continues until the team has all 22 pennies on the plate.

Say:

Each time someone gives 22 cents, another child gets a meal. Think about ways that your group could come up with 22 cents or more and how many children it would feed.

Block Walk
MUSICAL BLOCKS

"Junk" Needed:
Concrete blocks
Die
Large black permanent marker
Source of music

Resource Preparation:

Prepare and number a set of six questions about the story being taught. Write each number on two concrete blocks. Then, add some blocks that are blank.

You've heard of a cakewalk; well, this is a block walk. This twist to an old activity really creates some interest with kids.

Resource Fun:

- Place the concrete blocks in a circle. They should be spaced so that moving from one to the other requires a moderate leg stretch, so consider the age of the children playing.
- To begin the game, the children each choose a block to stand on.
- When the music starts to play, they should take long strides to move to the next block.
- When the music stops, one player will be chosen to roll the die.
- Whoever is on the block with that number is the one chosen to respond to the corresponding question.
- Since there are two sets of each number, two children could be on the same number.
- The question is asked to whichever child can answer first.
- That numbered question is now out of play, so if it comes up on the roll of the die, roll again.

If you have a large group of children, simply make additional sets of the six concrete blocks and add a few more blank ones.

Gather the Sheep
COTTON BALL CHIN-UPS

"Junk" Needed:
Cotton balls
Wide-mouth jar

This activity can be used with any story that mentions sheep and the shepherd. Review the responsibilities of the shepherd. He makes sure the sheep are in the fold where they can be protected from wild animals and from wandering off; he treats the sheep for any wounds they may have incurred; he leads them to green pasture and fresh water.

Resource Fun:

* The cotton balls will represent the sheep. The jar is the fold, and the child is the shepherd.
* The object of this game is to get as many cotton balls as possible in the jar, or sheep in the fold.
* The children will play in pairs.
* One child will be the shepherd, while the other child is the coach and judge.
* The shepherd is given ten cotton balls (sheep) to get in the fold (jar).
* Place the jar on the floor in front of the shepherd.
* At the signal, the child who is the shepherd will hold a cotton ball on his chin and try to drop it in the jar.
* The coach will give suggestions to help the shepherd position himself better to get the cotton ball in the jar.
* When all ten cotton balls have been dropped, count the sheep to determine how many sheep actually got in the fold.
* Repeat so the children can switch roles.

Say:

* The shepherd counted the sheep as they entered the fold, so he knew if any of the sheep were missing.
* Were some of your sheep missing from your fold?

Choosing a Volunteer
CRAFT STICK LOTS

"Junk" Needed:
Craft sticks
Permanent marker
Potato chip can

Trying to be fair and wanting *everyone* to get an opportunity to contribute?

Resource Preparation & Fun:

- Write the name of each child on a craft stick.
- Place all the sticks in a potato chip can that has been decorated for the season, unit, or class name.
- When you've asked for a volunteer and hands have gone up all over the room, draw out one of the craft sticks and you've solved the dilemma of choosing.

Toss and Scoop
GALLON JUG MEMORY GAME

"Junk" Needed:

Two, 1-gallon plastic milk jugs for each pair of kids

Tennis ball

To help your students learn the books of the Bible, use this game to inject some physical activity—making recitation a little more enthusiastic.

Resource Preparation & Fun #1:

- Cut the bottoms out of the gallon plastic milk jugs.
- Then, cut the plastic in a scoop fashion down toward the handle.
- The children will play in pairs; each child needs a milk jug scoop.
- Before beginning the actual game, allow the children some time to get used to tossing a tennis ball back and forth, catching it in the milk jug scoop rather than with their hands.
- When the children have figured out how to toss and scoop, then begin the game.
- The first child who scoops the tennis ball will say the first book of the Bible.
- Then, he tosses it back to the other child who says the second book of the Bible when he scoops the ball.
- The object is to try to toss and scoop as quickly as possible without missing one of the books or the tennis ball.
- Kids can act as each other's coach when a book is missed or pronounced incorrectly.

If the pair playing together gets stumped at a certain point, pause the game and let them refresh their memory by reviewing the Table of Contents of the Bible. Then, resume play and see if they can go a little further than they did previously.

Resource Fun #2:

- Substitute the milk jug scoops with 2, 1-gallon ice cream buckets.
- Toss the tennis ball high in the air as you begin.
- When it hits the bottom of the bucket it will bounce out.
- This variation goes much quicker than the milk jug scoop, because the ball never stops and hands never touch the ball after the game begins.
- Children playing this variation really have to know their books well.

Giant Ring Toss

BIBLE DRILLS

"Junk" Needed:

2 sets of Bible verse cards

6 Hula Hoops

Bibles

Carpet roll posts

New Hula Hoop for prize (optional)

Score pad (optional)

Starting lines

This is an exercise for *learning how to use the Bible* that can be used along with the story of Jonah, but doesn't have to be. If using with Jonah, tell the children that Jonah told the men on the boat that the only way for the storm to stop was to throw him overboard. We're going to throw some Hula Hoops overboard today and hope they get caught on a post.

Resource Preparation & Fun:

- Mount old carpet rolls (obtained free from carpet retailers) onto 2-foot square pieces of board so they will stand on their own.
- Cut the carpet rolls different lengths. (These can be painted and used for palm trees when not in use for this game. Stick an artificial fern in the top of the carpet roll and voila! It's a palm tree.)
- For this activity, though, the carpet rolls are giant tossing posts.
- Prepare a set of cards that have verses for the children to practice looking up. Include both Old and New Testament verses.
- Place the carpet roll posts in the yard about 4 feet from one another.
- Determine a stand-behind line where the kids will throw from.
- Each child will get three chances to throw a Hula Hoop at the posts.
- For each Hula Hoop that goes over a post, the player gets two points and an opportunity to find the verse from one of the cards.
- If they get two Hula Hoops over the posts, then they choose two cards and get two more points.
- When they find the verse(s), they should show their work to an adult who will then give them three additional points.

Optional:

To add a little extra fun…when the time is up, whoever has the highest score receives a new Hula Hoop to keep.

Tibetan Toss
RING A PRIZE

"Junk" Needed:
A few candy bars
Hula Hoops
Small toys
Wrapped candy

Tibetan Toss is a version of a game played by the children in Tibet and can be used as *a story reinforcement activity* to check the children's comprehension of the story you are focusing on.

Resource Preparation:
Prepare a set of questions about the story reflecting on both what happened and what was felt by those mentioned and write each one on a slip of paper.

Resource Fun:
- This game is best played outside, but can be used in a very large room.
- Scatter some small toys or wrapped candy on the lawn and tape one of the questions to each of them.
- Add a couple of extra toys or candy bars that have a slip of paper attached with **FREE** on them.
- These prizes should be large enough to be easily seen from a distance. (Check out the local dollar stores for inexpensive prizes.)
- Children will take turns tossing a Hula Hoop out on the lawn from a designated place in the center of the area where the prizes have been placed.
- If the Hula Hoop lands so that the prize is completely inside the hoop, then the players are asked the question attached to the prize.
- If they can answer the question correctly, then the prize is theirs to keep.
- If they can't answer the question, then they leave the prize there for the rest of the game.
- If the Hula Hoop goes over a prize that has a **FREE** tag on it, then the prize is theirs to keep, without having to answer a question.

Triple Tumble

PETER, DO YOU LOVE ME?

"Junk" Needed:

Hula Hoop

The Main Thing – Mark 14:66-72

Add this activity when studying the *story of Jesus challenging Peter three times* (Mark 14:66-72). Not once, not twice, but three times Jesus asked Peter, "Do you love me?" The point of the story will be accentuated while developing critical large motor skills.

Resource Fun:

- Choose 3 children (or other leaders) to hold 3 Hula Hoops upright, about 6 inches off the ground.

- Space the Hula Hoops about 6 feet apart.

- The first child will go to the first Hula Hoop, jump through it and do a somersault.

- When he or she stands up, the person holding the Hula Hoop will say, "Do you love me?"

- The player will respond, "Peter said, 'Yes, I love you.'"

- Then, the child moves to the second Hula Hoop, jumps through it and does a somersault, just like before.

- Again, the person holding the Hula Hoop will say, "Do you love me?" and the player will respond, "Peter said, 'Yes, I love you.'"

- Do this three times, just like Jesus asked Peter three times if he loved Him.

- Each child will complete all three hoops before starting the next child through the hoops.

Homemade Rubber Stamps

STAMP A STORY

"Junk" Needed:

Blocks of wood

Ink pad

Old inner tubes

Resource Preparation:

Can't find a rubber stamp that's exactly what you want? Wrong size? Wrong shape? Too expensive?

- Cut some scraps of 2" x 4" planks in 4" squares and sand the edges.
- Then, cut the figure you want on the stamp out of an inner tube.
- Adhere the figure onto the wooden block with rubber cement and let it dry thoroughly.

Resource Fun:

The children can use these rubber stamps in a variety of ways.

- Press them on an inkpad and transfer the pattern onto the surface.
- Or, use a sponge brush to paint a very light coat of craft paint on the pattern to transfer.
- If the pattern of the stamp is a geometric shape, the children can create a stained glass window picture to portray a scene in the story they are studying.
- Make a sheep stamp and mount a large piece of green paper on the wall.
- The children can paint the stamps with white paint and create the scene of 99 sheep and the one lost.
- Make a set of alphabet rubber stamps for the kids to print out their scripture memory verse or key words they have learned using the alphabet stamps.
- If an inner tube isn't available, cut the figures from Styrofoam™ meat trays and adhere them to a wood block to make a stamp.

Ten Commandment Bumpers

INNER TUBE SCRAMBLE

To add an energy-releaser for the children as they learn the *Ten Commandments*, incorporate this activity into the lesson. Before beginning the activity, review the Ten Commandments (Exodus 20:3-17) and the number associated with each of them.

Resource Preparation & Fun:

- Use white paint to write the numbers 1-10 on ten of the inner tubes.
- The other (11th) inner tube is plain.
- Put a child inside each of the inner tubes and instruct the ones with the numbers to spread out and stand still.
- The child who has the inner tube without the number will be the bumper.
- If that child knows the commandments, he or she will run up to that number inner tube and bump the child in it.
- When he or she bumps, then the child (the bumper) has to recite the commandment belonging to that number.
- If he is correct, he can go to another numbered inner tube and bump it.
- The bumper does not have to go in order.
- He can continue bumping until he gets a commandment wrong, or voluntarily says he doesn't know any more.
- When one person is finished being the bumper, then choose another child to be the bumper.
- Give a signal and all the other kids in the inner tubes have to change inner tubes.

The kids love playing with these bumpers, but do give the warning when the game begins that anyone getting too rough will have to sit out for at least one round.

Jacob's Ladder
BEAN THE CUPS

The Main Thing – Genesis 27:42—29:12

While learning about Jacob's dream in the desert the kids will love playing this game. After Jacob tricked Esau out of his blessing, Jacob fled. He wandered through the wilderness and was very lonely. As night came, Jacob found a rock to use as a pillow and drifted off to sleep. He dreamed he saw angels going up and down a ladder to heaven. Jacob saw God standing at the top of the ladder. In the dream God assured Jacob that He would take care of him, and that the land he was sleeping on would one day become the land where Jacob's people would live. God also told Jacob that his descendants would be as many as the dust on the earth.

"Junk" Needed:

Beanbag
Ladder
Masking tape
White cups

Resource Preparation & Fun #1:

- Prepare a set of questions about the story.
- Set up a ladder and place an upside-down white cup on each rung.
- About eight feet back from the ladder put down a piece of masking tape for children to line up behind.
- Kids will take turns tossing a beanbag at the ladder, trying to knock one of the cups off.
- If they are successful, ask them a question about the story.

Resource Fun #2:

- Make the children knock the cups off in order, from the bottom rung to the top.
- If a cup on a different rung is knocked off, it has to be replaced.

Game Board

WHAT SHOULD YOU DO?

Resource Preparation:

- Mark off 1" squares on a square of linoleum tile.
- The squares should entirely cover the tile.
- Paint the squares in different shades of one color using acrylic craft paints, except for 10 squares that are randomly scattered around the board. Paint these 10 squares white.
- Once the paint is dry, outline the squares once again with a black permanent marker.
- Give the board one coat of polyurethane to keep the paint from chipping. (Believe me, there are people in your church who don't feel like they can work in children's ministry, but they would love to paint these boards! Seek them out and let them have a ball!)
- Prepare a set of **"What Should You Do?"** questions for the game cards.
- Write each situation on a small piece of cardstock. The cards should have situations like: As you walk out of the store, you realize the cashier gave you too much change. What should you do?
- You will need one board and one set of situation cards for each pair of children.

Resource Fun:

- Give each pair of children a game board, a set of cards, a red checker and a black checker.

- Each child gets a checker as his or her marker and can place it anywhere on the board as a starting point, but at least 3 squares from a white square.

- Each child also gets 10 M&Ms™ (all in one color). Each player should have different color M&Ms™.

- The first player rolls the die and can then move his or her checker that number of spaces forward, backward, to the sides, **but not diagonally**.

- Players can also turn a corner in the middle of their move.

- The object is to land on one of the white squares. In order to land on one of the white squares, a player must have the exact number on the die.

- If the player is successful in landing on a white square, he or she draws a situation card and responds to it.

- The player then keeps the card and places a piece of his or her candy on the square as a marker, along with his or her checker.

- The M&M™ remains on the square the rest of the game, although the player moves his or her checker on the next turn. That square is now out of play, and the other player takes a turn.

- The object is to get all 10 white squares out of play.

- When the game is over, clean up is easy…just eat the markers!

Easter Grid
ROAD TO THE CROSS

"Junk" Needed:
5 pieces of paper
Large foam die
Masking tape

Resource Preparation:

- Create a 12-foot square with masking tape.
- Now, turn the square into a grid by putting strips of masking tape every foot going both directions. You can make the grid larger than this, but don't make it smaller.
- Make five signs on scrap paper that read:
  - Jesus eats with His disciples.
  - Jesus goes to the garden to pray.
  - Jesus is arrested.
  - Jesus is hung on the cross.
  - Jesus is buried in a grave.
- Tape the signs randomly on five squares of the grid.

Jesus is arrested.

Resource Fun:

- Each child will choose any square on the edge of the grid to be his or her personal starting place.
- Players will take turns tossing the die to find out how many squares they can move their game pieces—themselves.
- They can move forward, backward, or sideways, *but not diagonally*.
- The object is to travel through the signs in the correct order (as listed above) by moving the number rolled on the die.
- They will move towards the sign that reads, "Jesus eats with His disciples" first.
- As they travel through each sign, they need to say what is written on it out loud.
- After they have passed "Jesus was buried in a grave" they finish the game by rolling enough to take them one step out of the grid. It must be an exact roll.
- Once they step outside the grid the players shout, "Jesus rose from the dead!"

"Junk" Needed:

Masking tape

Ball

Scraps of paper

Resource Preparation:

- Make a grid of 16 squares (4 squares x 4 squares) on the floor using masking tape. The squares should be uniform, 1-2 foot squares.

- Write the numbers 1-16 on pieces of scrap paper.

- Tape one piece of scrap paper in each of the squares in random order.

- About 6 feet away from the grid, place a piece of masking tape for kids to stand behind.

- Prepare a set of 16 questions about the story and number them.

- If there aren't 16 questions to ask, prepare 8 questions and repeat them twice.

Resource Fun:

- Players take turns standing at the line and bouncing the ball, trying to get it to land in square number one.

- Once number one is hit, the number one question is asked of that player.

- Now, players will try to bounce the ball in square number two.

- Continue going through the numbers until all 16 questions have been asked.

- If a player is unable to answer the question, the next player to hit that number will attempt to answer the question.

Orderly Dismissal

KID TOSS

"Junk" Needed:
Masking tape

Do the kids rush out the door in chaos? Are papers and projects left behind? Did you miss giving a child an encouraging hug? Are parents wondering where their child is?

Resource Preparation & Fun:

Use this simple little trick to add some order to dismissal time.

- With masking tape, mark a box the width of the door and about two feet deep on the floor.
- The box blocks the entrance to the room now.
- Tell children that this is the teacher's box, and when it is time to dismiss, they are not allowed to enter the box.
- The teacher can see parents in the hallway, call a child to the box, make sure he or she has everything brought to class and everything from the class time, and be able to get a good-bye hug.
- And then, if you want to "throw your kids out of class," pick each one up as he or she leaves and swing him or her out the door!
- A few pieces of masking tape not only provide order, but also create a special moment for each child as he or she leaves.

Tic-Tac-Toe
TWELVE QUESTIONS IN A ROW

"Junk" Needed:

Masking tape

Post-It® notes

Poster board

Resource Preparation:

- Mark off a large tic-tac-toe grid with bright-colored masking tape on a wall.
- Construct 12 questions about the story being taught.
- Write these on squares of poster board that will fit into the grid.
- Tape nine of the poster board squares on the tic-tac-toe board with the question face down.

Resource Fun:

- Form two groups of players. One group will be "O" and the other "X".
- Give each team five Post-It® notes that have its marking ("X" or "O") on them.
- The team with a player whose birthday is closest to Christmas begins the game.
- One player from a team will choose a block on the tic-tac-toe grid and try to answer the question from the poster board square found on that block.
- If the player answers correctly, he or she will remove the poster board and place one of the Post-It® notes displaying their marking ("O" or "X") in the block. (The player must position the Post-It® on the tic-tac-toe board without input from teammates.)
- If they cannot answer the question then they can ask their team members.
- If the team cannot answer, then the question is removed and replaced with one of the extra questions and play moves on without a Post-It® being placed on the board.
- The game is over when one of the teams gets three of its Post-It® notes in a row: vertically, horizontally, or diagonally.

Variation:

- Number the blocks on the tic-tac-toe grid.
- Put corresponding slips of paper in a container.
- Draw one of the numbers out of the container—that will be the block the teams are playing for.
- Each team will choose one player to represent them.
- The leader asks the question and whichever player answers correctly first gets to mark the block for their team with a Post-It® note.

Funky Giant Crayons

CAN YOU COLOR THE MUFFIN MAN?

So, you're thinking about throwing all the crayons out and starting over? Before you do that try making these unique giant crayons.

Resource Fun:

- The children will take the paper off of old crayons that are no longer being used because they are broken or worn down.
- Put the broken pieces in muffin tins. Similar colors can be put together or put a variety of colors in one tin.
- Place the muffin tin in a hot oven, and leave it there until the crayons have completely melted.
- Let the pan cool and then pop out some funky crayons.
- The children will now have giant rainbow crayons that are different than anything they've ever colored with.

Use the giant crayons to draw on newsprint to recreate a Bible story.

"Junk" Needed:

Muffin pans

Old crayons

Muffin Pan Trap
PING-PONG QUESTIONS

"Junk" Needed:

Masking tape

Muffin pans

Ping-Pong balls

Red construction paper

Resource preparation:

- Gather as many muffin pans as you can.
- Push them all together on the floor in a large square (or irregular shape), but make sure some are against a wall.
- Cut out at least one red construction paper circle to go in a cup of each muffin pan.
- Secure those red circles with a loop of tape.

Resource Fun:

- Mark a stand-behind line for the children. Depending on the type of floor the game is placed on, the stand-behind line may need to be closer or further away from the muffin pans. (A hard floor will make the balls bounce more easily, so the line should be further back.)
- One player at a time will gently toss a ping-pong ball on the floor so that it will bounce towards the muffin pans.
- If it gets trapped in one of the cups with a red circle, the player gets a point, and also an opportunity to respond.
- The response can be to a question about the story, a "What would you do?" situation question that goes along with the topic of the lesson or a chance to recite a scripture memory verse.
- Ping-pong balls have a high bounce quality, so remind kids of that as they take their turns.
- The player with the most points at the end of the game gets to toss all the ping-pong balls at once at the muffin pans! Now, that's fun!

Paper Clips
MAGNETIC GLEANING

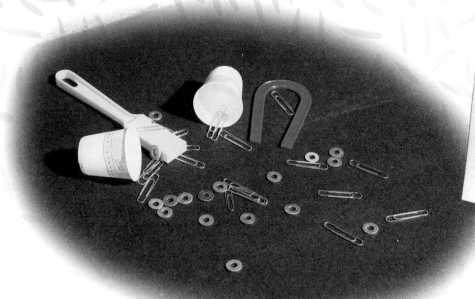

"Junk" Needed:

Magnets
Paper clips
Small cups
Washers (and other little metal objects)

The Main Thing – Ruth 1—4

Ruth picked up grain to feed herself and her mother-in-law, Naomi. The pieces of grain that she picked up were very small and Ruth had to bend over all day to get enough grain to feed the two of them.

Resource Fun:

- Spread the paper clips, washers, and other small metal objects all over the floor to represent the grain left after the workers had picked the field.
- Give each child a magnet and a small cup.
- At the signal, the children will see how many paper items they can put in their cup, using the magnet.

If you have plenty of little metal objects but lack the magnets, they can be purchased from www.discountschoolsupply.com.

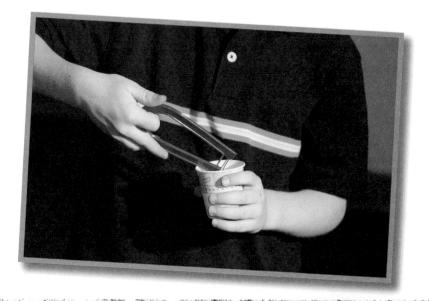

Pass It On
IT ONLY TAKES A PING-PONG BALL

"Junk" Needed:

2 cardboard paper towel rollers for each child

One ping-pong ball

Resource Fun:

- The children will position themselves close together, side-by-side, in a long line. The line doesn't necessarily have to be straight.
- Give each of the children two cardboard paper towel rollers to hold, one in each hand.
- The kids will be connecting their paper towel rollers end-to-end, so that when the ping-pong ball is placed in the very end, it will be able to travel through the entire tube.
- But, the children are not allowed to position their paper towel roller until the ping-pong ball is only two people away.
- When the ball gets to the other end, encourage everyone to go to the end and give everyone high fives! Now, discuss the following questions.

The Main Thing

Ask:

- How did you have to handle your paper towel roller in order for the ball to successfully pass through?
- How did you feel when the ball went through your tubes successfully?
- What were your feelings about the people who came after you?
- How was this exercise like the message of Jesus being passed on to our friends and neighbors?
- How do you feel when someone you know receives Jesus into his or her life?
- Can we afford to be sloppy with the way we handle the Word of God?
- After we were successful at passing along the ping-pong ball, what did our celebration remind you of?
- When we tell others about Jesus, or when they watch how we live, we need to be very careful about what we say and do.
- Jesus should be such a part of our lives that passing on His message is something we concentrate on.
- When friends or people in our family give lives over to God, we're excited, because God's message went through us to them. When we all get to heaven, we'll celebrate with those who brought the message to us and with those who received the message because we passed it on!

Walk in My Shoes
ARMOR OF GOD

Resource Preparation:

- The children should take off their shoes and place the heels against the wall, so that shoes are side-by-side and touching.
- Place a masking tape stand-behind-line about 3 feet from the shoes.

Resource Fun:

- Each player will take a turn at tossing the ping-pong ball at the shoes.
- If the ball goes in a shoe, the person who owns the shoe will respond by suggesting a way we can follow Jesus.
- Once the shoe has been hit, it is taken out of the game and returned to its owner.

The Main Thing

The Bible also speaks of the shoes of peace when talking about the armor of God (Ephesians 6:10-17). If you use the game with a lesson on the armor of God, ask the children to respond with ways they can be peacemakers in situations they face each day.

"Junk" Needed:
Masking tape
Ping-Pong balls
Shoes

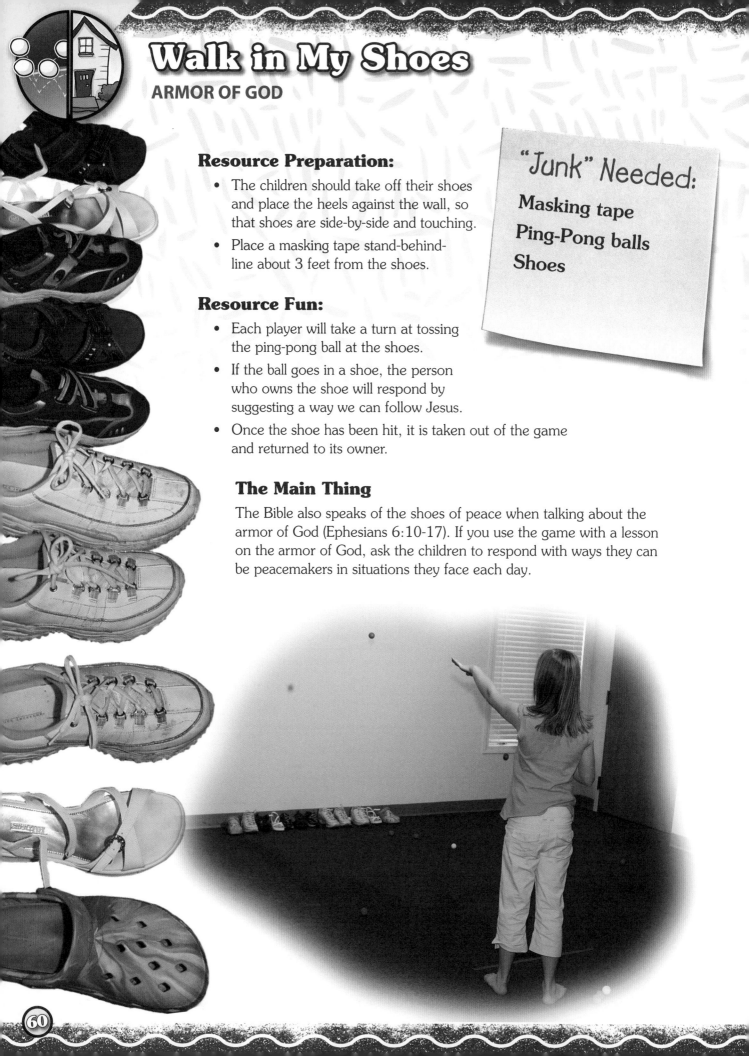

Where's Baby Moses?

PING-PONG HUNT

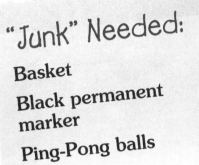

"Junk" Needed:

Basket

Black permanent marker

Ping-Pong balls

The Main Thing – Exodus 1:1—2:10

The Pharaoh was concerned about the growing number of Israelites. These people were his slaves and it wouldn't be long before there were more Israelites than Egyptians. So Pharaoh came up with a plan and declared a new rule that all the baby boys should be killed. Moses' mother came up with a plan of her own to hide baby Moses. She prepared a basket to put Moses in and sent it with Miriam, Moses' sister. Miriam took the basket to the water's edge and placed it among the reeds. When Pharaoh's daughter came to the water to bathe, she found the basket and eventually took baby Moses back to the palace to rear as her own son. Moses was not harmed by Pharaoh or his new plan. God had protected baby Moses.

Resource Preparation:

Children love to search out and find hidden objects.

- Prepare a large supply of ping-pong balls by drawing simple faces on about half of them with a black permanent marker.
- If the weather permits, hide all the ping-pong balls outside (both the ones with faces and the blank ones); otherwise, find good hiding places indoors.

Resource Fun:

- Instruct the children what the boundaries are for looking, then let them search for the ping-pong balls.
- When a ball with a face on it is discovered, the child should yell, "The princess found baby Moses" and then bring the ball to the basket.
- If a blank one is found, set those aside in a separate pile.

Sit and Scoot
MOVING QUESTIONS

Resource:

- Plant caddies are the little platforms on wheels that are used to move large plants from one place to another.
- Scooters used for gym class can be purchased from a recreational equipment company for about $40 each.
- Plant caddies are basically the same thing, usually run about $8, and can support up to 180 pounds.
- Check with plant lovers because they probably have some extras stashed in their garage.

Resource Preparation & Fun:

- Prepare a set of questions and put them on individual cards.
- Place the cards on the ground about 30 feet away from the starting point.
- Plant scooters will work on tile, wood, pavement and even low pile carpeting.
- Instruct the children to sit on the scooters and propel themselves backwards by pushing with their feet.
- When they get to the question cards, each child will grab a card and return to the starting line.
- Pause to answer the questions before moving on to the next two children.
- After all the children have had an opportunity to participate, then do the activity again, only allowing the children to decide how they'll sit, lay or push the scooter.
- No standing allowed.

Variation:

- Tie a 10-foot rope to each scooter and let partners pull one another.
- The distance needs to be increased for this because the scooters will go much faster.

Who's Got the Egg?

PETER SAYS "NO"

"Junk" Needed:
One plastic egg

The Main Thing – Matthew 26:69-75; Mark 14:66-72; Luke 22:55-62; John 18:25-27

This activity is intended to reinforce the story of Peter's denial that he was a follower of Jesus. *(Excerpt from Egermeier's® Bible Story Book ©2007 Warner Press, Inc All rights reserved.)*

The soldiers brought Jesus to the house of Annas, and here the trial began. As Peter stood in the courtyard, a young girl said, "Are you not also one of his disciples?"

Peter was afraid and said, "No, I do not know the man." Peter went to the fire to warm himself. Around the fire stood other men, the high priest's servants and some soldiers. One turned to Peter and asked, "Are you not one of this man's disciples?" Again fear filled Peter's heart, and he replied, "No, I am not!"

A soldier standing by who had seen Peter use his sword said, "I saw you in the garden with him!" Peter cursed and said, "I know not the man!"

Meanwhile the high priest and others had been questioning Jesus and treating him shamefully. They led Jesus away. As he passed by, he looked sadly at Peter. Now Peter remembered Jesus' words, "Before the cock crows, you will deny me three times." Peter turned blindly away from the fire, rushed out and wept bitterly.

Three times Peter told different people that he wasn't with Jesus. Why would Peter do such a thing? What did Peter say each time someone asked, "Aren't you the one who was with him?" (Peter said, "No, not me!")

Resource Fun:

- The children will sit in a circle.
- Choose one child to stand in the middle and close his or her eyes.
- The children will pass around one plastic egg behind their backs.
- When the person in the middle crows, the egg stops.
- The player in the center will count to three and then open his or her eyes.
- While the person in the middle is counting to three, the player who has the egg will hide it behind his or her back.
- When the player in the center opens his eyes, he will try to choose who has the egg.
- If he chooses incorrectly, the player he chose will say, "Peter said, 'No, not me!'"
- Remind the children frequently that Peter replied "No, not me" several times when asked if he was a follower of Jesus.
- Keep choosing until the child in the middle finds the person with the egg.
- The person with the egg becomes the next player to stand in the middle and guess where the egg is.

Jonathan's Warning
HOOP & NOODLES

"Junk" Needed:
Hula Hoop
Pool noodle
Rope

The Main Thing – 1 Samuel 20

Playing this game will help reinforce the story of Jonathan warning David about the threatening King Saul. In the story Jonathan shoots an arrow a long distance and tells the boy who is with him, "The arrow is beyond you." That was David's cue that he should flee from King Saul.

Resource Fun:

- Hang a Hula Hoop from a tree with the rope, so that the hoop is suspended about eye level for the children.
- Determine a stand-behind line from which the pool noodle will be thrown. As the children throw the pool noodle, the line distance may need to be adjusted.
- The children take turns throwing the pool noodle, trying to get it to go through the Hula Hoop.
- When they are successful at getting the noodle to go through, they respond with the warning phrase that Jonathan gave David, "The arrow is beyond you!"

Ask:

- How do you think David felt when he found out that King Saul was threatening to kill him?
- What made Jonathan's decision to help David a difficult one?
- What do you think David thought of his friend, Jonathan, for helping him in this way?

How Many Times Should We Forgive?

POPCORN RELAY

"Junk" Needed:

7 popcorn boxes for each group

Big supply of popcorn

Large container for popcorn

Small cup

The Main Thing – Matthew 18:21-25

In Matthew 18:21-25 Peter is learning about forgiveness. Jesus told him a story to demonstrate that his forgiveness should be beyond any number he could think of. Sometimes, we get weary in forgiving others, but Jesus encourages us to never stop forgiving the people who have wronged us. To get a physical idea of how many times that may be, play this relay game.

Resource Fun:

- Form groups of 6-10 kids and give each a small cup.
- Place the large container of popcorn in a central location where all groups have equal access to it.
- About 20 feet away from each group, position 7 popcorn boxes for that group.
- When the leader gives the signal, one kid from each group will fill his or her small cup and take it to the popcorn boxes where he or she will fill the boxes with popcorn.
- That player returns to the group with the empty cup and passes it on to another team member, who will refill the cup with popcorn. Continue carrying small cups of popcorn to the 7 boxes until the leader determines that one group has filled all its boxes.

Say:

- Let's count the seven full containers of the winning group out loud.
- Should we forgive 7 times? No, we should forgive more times than there is popcorn in the containers!
- Is that a little or a lot? There's more popcorn in these boxes than I want to count. I'm not even sure I could eat all this popcorn!
- Let's pour the popcorn back into the original container. That's a lot of popcorn!
- God wants us to forgive more times than we can count!

Name the Disciples
PVC & TENNIS BALL RACE

"Junk" Needed:

1½" diameter
PVC pipe, 30" long

1½" diameter
PVC elbow

12 tennis balls

Buckets

Memorizing the names of all 12 disciples can be quite a chore, but it's a helpful and important thing everyone needs to know as they study the New Testament. Take the chore out of learning them by using this fun game to come up with the names of all 12 disciples.

Resource Fun:

- Right before beginning the game, review the names of Jesus' disciples.
- Push the PVC elbow onto the end of the PVC pipe.
- Place a bucket (ice cream stores and delis get rid of plastic buckets all the time) about 30 feet away.
- One child at a time will hold the end of the PVC pipe so that the end with the elbow is out away from his body.
- There should be 12 tennis balls at the start line.
- The first child will place a tennis ball on the elbow and balance it there by holding the other end.
- When the player gets to the bucket, he has to call out one of the names of the disciples, and then drop the tennis ball in the bucket.
- If he can't name a disciple, then he has to take the tennis ball off the PVC and carry it back to the rest of the group.
- Once a disciple has been named, no one else can use that name.
- Continue playing until all 12 tennis balls (disciples) are in the bucket.

Pick Up the Wreckage

PAUL IS SHIPWRECKED

"Junk" Needed:

Craft sticks

Old sheet

The Main Thing – Acts 27

Use this activity with the story of Paul being shipwrecked.

(Excerpt from Egermeier's® Bible Story Book ©2007 Warner Press, Inc All rights reserved.)

The sea beat against the back of the ship so violently that the ship began to break up. The soldiers wanted to kill their prisoners for fear some would escape. If one got away, a soldier would have to pay with his own life. The Roman captain did not want Paul killed, so he refused to let the soldiers harm any of the prisoners.

At the captain's orders those who could swim jumped into the water and swam to shore. Others found broken pieces of the ship and floated ashore. Not one of the two hundred and seventy-six people was drowned.

Resource Fun:

- Lay a big handful of craft sticks on the ground that represents the wreckage of the ship.
- Place an old sheet over the top to represent the sea.
- Choose two kids to stand one step back from the sheet.
- All the others will hold onto the edge of the sheet.
- As the leader says, "The storm was getting rougher and rougher," the children will move the sheet to resemble a stormy sea.
- Then the leader will say, "The boat Paul was on broke apart!"
- That's the signal for the children to raise the sheet in the air.

- As they do this, the two players that have been waiting will rush under the sheet to pick up as many craft sticks as they can before the sheet comes back down on top of them.
- Alternate the children who get to run under the sheet until *everyone* who wants to participate has an opportunity to do so.

Pull Jeremiah from the Well

TUG A PROPHET

The Main Thing – Jeremiah 38:1-13

Jeremiah spoke the truth about God and warned the people that terrible things would happen to them because they were not pleasing God. Some of the people got so angry they threw Jeremiah into a well. He would've died there, but the king sent men to pull him out. They tied rags together to make ropes and let them down into the well. Did you know the Bible mentions armpits? Jeremiah tied the rag-ropes under his armpits and was pulled out of the well.

Resource Preparation:

- Tear the old sheets into full-length strips about 6" wide.
- Using the largest piece of scrap plywood available, cut it into the shape of a person.
- Position the shape on the wood so that the cut-out has some space as armpits.

Resource Fun:

- Time the children to see how fast they can get Jeremiah out of the well.
- Place the wooden cut-out as far away as possible (perhaps at the other end of the parking lot or hallway).
- When the leader starts the stopwatch, the children must work together to tie the sheeting strips together so they reach from where they are standing to where the Jeremiah figure is laying.
- When they've tied enough strips together to reach Jeremiah, then tie the end under his armpits to secure him.
- The children will then pull Jeremiah from where he is to the place where they were originally standing.
- As they are working, keep encouraging them to get Jeremiah out of the well.
- If you have a large group of children, use about six at a time and compare their times.

"Junk" Needed:
Old sheets
Scrap of plywood
Stopwatch

Sheet Game Board
QUESTIONS AND A DIE

"Junk" Needed:
Large foam die
Old sheet
Permanent markers

Resource Preparation:

- With a pencil, draw a winding trail of large blocks on the sheet to resemble a game board. (Check out games like Chutes and Ladders™ and Candyland™ to see how they are laid out.) There's no wrong or right way; just make sure there is a beginning and an end.

- Color the blocks different colors with permanent markers, interspersing one red block quite often (every 3-5 blocks).

- Making the game board would be a fun project for the kids when they are just hanging out together.

Resource Fun:

- The kids will choose something in the room to be their marker. (This could be an eraser, shoe, pencil, vegetable can.)

- Once they have their marker, they'll take turns rolling the die and moving their marker.

- If they land on a red square, they must respond to something that goes along with the lesson. This can be a question about the story, a multiple choice question, a situation response "What would you do?" or reciting the memory verse.

A High Tower

TOWER OF BABEL

"Junk" Needed:

Large supply of shoe boxes

Packing tape

The Main Thing – Genesis 9:18—11:9

This activity will grab the attention of the kids and get them actively involved when teaching about the Tower of Babel.

Resource Preparation:

- Collect empty shoe boxes until you have a huge number of them. The more boxes you have, the more fun the activity will be.

- Discount department stores that display their shoes on racks, rather than in boxes, are willing to give away their boxes. Just arrange a time with them for pick up.

- There is no need for the boxes to all be the same size.

- Prepare the boxes for this activity by wrapping one strip of packing tape around them to keep the lids on securely.

The Main Thing...

After the flood waters went down, Noah and the animals got off the ark. When the world was populated again, the people decided to build a city. In the city they wanted to make a tower that was so high it would reach to the sky. They concentrated so hard on building the tower they thought less and less about God. How do you think God felt when He saw all the effort they were putting into building a tower?

Resource Fun:

- Show the children the supply of shoe boxes.
- They'll get excited just seeing this wealth of resources!
- Challenge them to build a tower as high as they can, using only the shoeboxes.
- Provide some small step stools for them to stand on in case the towers get taller than the kids.

Ask:

Did God knock down the tower? How did God stop the tower from being built?

Pancake Mania

CATCH A VERSE

"Junk" Needed:

Dinner plate

Poster board circles

Skillet

Spatula

Resource Preparation:

- Prepare a set of questions about the story you are studying.
- Then cut out a circle from the poster board, about the size of a pancake, for each question.
- Write the question on the poster board pancake.

Resource Fun:

- The children will take turns being the flipper and the catcher.
- The flipper will place a pancake in the skillet and slide the spatula underneath.
- The catcher will hold the plate and try to catch the pancake when it is tossed in the air.
- The way the pancake is tossed is that the flipper hits the handle of the spatula hard and quick in a downward motion. The pancake should fly in the air.
- Then, it's a mad dash by the catcher to follow the pancake and try to catch it on their plate without using their hands to keep it there.
- When the two are successful at flipping and catching, they read what is on their pancake and respond to the question.
- Each pair will get three tries at catching a pancake.

Clear the Temple
CARDS & SPOONS

"Junk" Needed:
Go Fish cards
Masking tape
Spoons

The Main Thing - John 2:13-17; Matthew 21:12-13

When Jesus went into the temple and saw the mini-marketplace that had been set up to buy sacrificial animals, He was enraged. He saw people doing things in God's house they shouldn't have been doing. The temple was supposed to be a place to worship God, but the people had made it into a place of business. When Jesus saw this, He turned over the tables and chased the people out of the temple.

Resource Preparation & Fun:

- With masking tape, make a 2-foot square in the center of the floor.
- Put a spoon for each child in the square, minus one.
- There will always be a spoon for all but one person.
- Give each child two Go Fish cards.
- At the signal, everyone will choose one card to pass to the person on his right.
- At the same time they are passing a card to the person to their right, the person on their left will be passing them a card.
- Each time the leader gives a signal, the children will pass another card.
- When someone is holding two identical cards, they will yell "Clear the temple!" and everyone will grab a spoon.
- There's no need for anyone to be eliminated...just enjoy playing together and clearing the temple.

Quirky Putt-Putt
A QUESTION IN ONE

"Junk" Needed:
Golf putter (toy or real)
Large Styrofoam™ cups
Old golf balls
Permanent marker

Resource Preparation:
- Cut the bottom out of 10-15 large Styrofoam™ cups.
- Number the cups on the side with a permanent marker.
- Prepare a set of questions about the lesson being taught and number them to match the numbers on the cups.

Resource Fun:
- Scatter the cups in the grass, laying them on their sides.
- Each player will swing the golf putter to make contact with the ball one time on his or her turn.
- Be aware it may take more than one swing to actually hit the ball.
- The next player goes to where the ball is and takes his swing.
- The object is to get the ball to completely pass through one of the cups.
- When a player does this, he or she will answer the matching question.
- If a player cannot answer the question, the ball will be placed next to the cup and the next player will take their swing, heading the ball toward a different cup.
- If the ball stops inside the cup, the leader will roll the ball back out of the cup and the next player will get to take a swing to get it all the way through.
- Pick up the cups once the question has been answered correctly.
- Continue doing this until all the cups have been picked up.

Hunt for the Lost Sheep
SAND & PEANUTS

The Main Thing –
Luke 15:3-7; Matthew 18:12-14

Jesus told a story about a shepherd who counted his sheep. He knew that he had 100 sheep, but when he counted them, there were only 99. The shepherd left the 99 that were safe in the fold to go out and find the one lost sheep. When he found the sheep he celebrated. God celebrates when one person who has not been following Him decides to come back to the God who created them and loves them so much.

"Junk" Needed:
Large tub
Play sand
Styrofoam™ peanuts

Resource
Preparation & Fun

- Count 100 Styrofoam™ peanuts.
- Color one of the peanuts bright red.
- Then place all the peanuts in a large tub of sand, so they are hidden.
- The children will take turns finding a Styrofoam™ peanut in the sand.
- They must pull out the first peanut they find or uncover.
- The shepherd in the story wouldn't stop looking until he found the one lost sheep.
- The children will keep pulling out the Styrofoam™ peanuts, one by one, until they locate the red one—the lost sheep.
- When it is found, everyone should yell, "He's back! He's back! The lost sheep is back!"

"Junk" Needed:

3 tap lights

Black permanent marker

Container

Milk caps

Resource Preparation:

So, you purchased some of those tap lights and never quite found a place to use them. Well, here's a way to make them into a great teaching tool.

- Make sure the tap lights have batteries in them before beginning the activity. (Tap lights can be purchased for a dollar at the dollar stores.)
- Prepare a set of questions that go along with the story being studied.
- Before beginning, each child will write his or her name on a milk cap and place it in the container.

Resource Fun

- Use three tap lights for this activity.
- Place the tap lights at the edge of a table.
- Draw out three milk caps to choose who will play each round.
- The three players will stand at the lights with their hands behind their backs.
- The leader will ask a question about the story.
- The first child to tap his or her light so that it turns on gets the opportunity to answer the question.
- Players must keep their hands behind their backs until the entire question has been read.
- Return the milk caps to the container and draw out three more caps for the players in the next question round.

A Pick Me Up

JACOB, LEAH & RACHEL

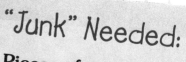

"Junk" Needed:

Pieces of poster board

Toilet plunger

The Main Thing – Genesis 29:13—31:55

This activity was designed to use with the lesson of Jacob. *(Excerpt from Egermeier's® Bible Story Book ©2007 Warner Press, Inc All rights reserved.)*

Jacob helped his uncle. By the end of the month Laban said, "Let me pay you for your work. How much do you want?"

Jacob replied, "I will serve you faithfully for seven years if then you will give me your beautiful daughter Rachel to be my wife." Jacob loved Rachel and wanted to marry her. He loved her so much that the seven years seemed like only a few days.

When the seven years were up, Jacob reminded his uncle of their agreement. Laban arranged a marriage feast and invited many friends to the wedding. In the evening he brought the bride to Jacob. A veil covered her face and no one could see her. This was the custom.

After the ceremony Jacob wanted to see his bride. He lifted the veil, but it was not the beautiful Rachel whom he loved. Instead it was her older sister, Leah. How unhappy he was! His uncle had tricked him. Perhaps Jacob remembered how he had tricked his blind father and cheated his brother out of the blessing.

Resource Preparation & Fun:

Prepare a set of questions about the story or use the ones provided here.

- Write each question on a separate piece of poster, about an 8" square.
- Lay the questions out on a hard surface, question side down.
- The children will take turns picking up a question by using the suction of the toilet plunger. This is a riot! And isn't it great to hear children laugh while they're learning!

You could also use this activity as a way of asking questions about any story.

Who was Jacob's uncle? (Laban)

What kind of work did Jacob do for Laban? (took care of his sheep)

Who was Jacob in love with? (Rachel)

Who was Rachel's father? (Laban)

Why was Jacob working for Laban? (so he could marry Rachel)

How many years did Jacob think he would have to work for Laban so he could marry Rachel? (7)

Who was Rachel's sister? (Leah)

Why did Laban trick Jacob into marrying Leah? (She was supposed to get married first, because she was the oldest.)

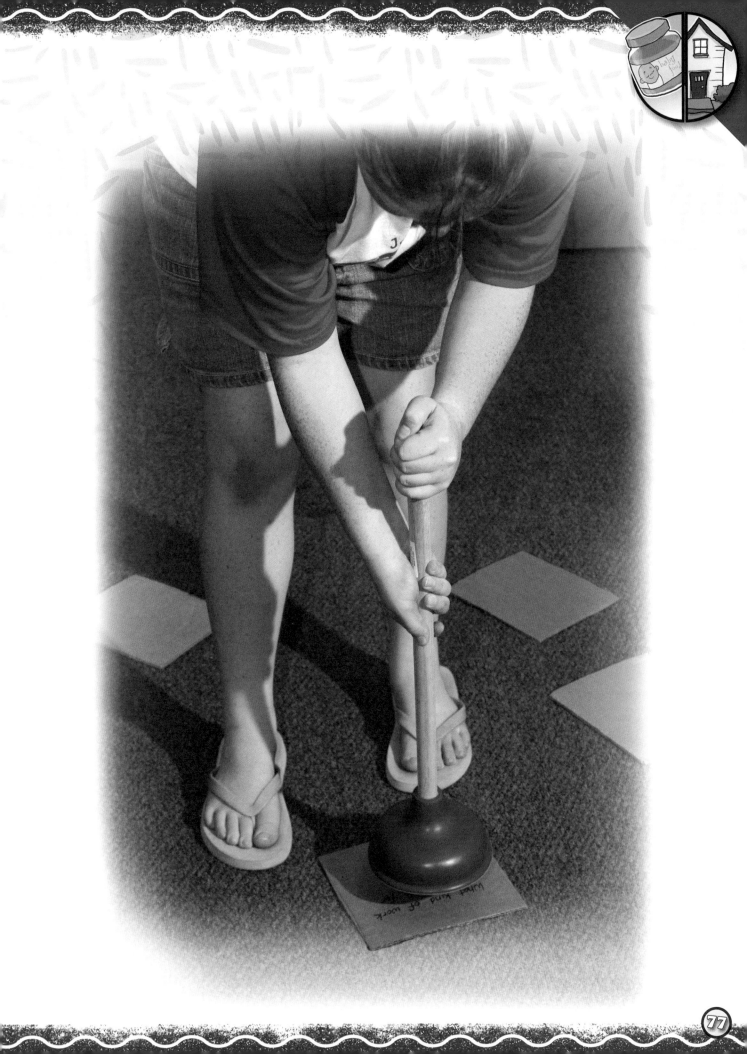

Creation Plunge
CATCH THE TENNIS BALL

This game is set up to play with the story of Creation, but is generic enough that it could be used with many other stories.

Remember the child's game of the cup that was on a stick and had a ball on the end of a string that was attached to it? The object of the game was to swing the ball on the string and try to catch it in the cup. This is a similar game, but only on a larger scale and with an object that's not usually considered a toy.

Resource Preparation:

- Drill a hole in the handle of a toilet plunger about 3" from where the rubber suction cup is attached to the handle.

- Thread the clothesline rope through the hole and knot the end of the rope. Make a big enough knot so the rope won't come through even if jerked on.

- Drill a hole through a tennis ball and thread the other end of the clothesline rope through it. Knot the end so the rope won't come through the ball.

Resource Fun:

- Allow each child 30 seconds to see if he or she can catch the tennis ball in the toilet plunger.

- Once the 30 seconds are over, the player passes the toilet plunger on to the next child who gets a 30-second turn to catch the tennis ball.

- When the first person is successful, he will tell what God created on the first day.

- The next person to successfully catch the ball tells what God created on the second day, and so forth.

- When all seven days have been identified, then start over with day one.

- Play as long as time allows and quit before your sides cramp from the laughter!

Trash Bag Altar
ELIJAH & THE PROPHETS OF BAAL

"Junk" Needed:
Newspaper

Rope or masking tape

Small plastic trashcan liners

The Main Thing – 1 Kings 18:17-40

The people who believed in the false god Baal challenged Elijah to see whose God would answer when the sacrifice was made. The prophets of Baal tried everything, but Baal would not answer. Elijah instructed the people to bring him 12 rough stones to build the altar to the One True God. Even though the stones had been drenched in water, God sent down fire from heaven to burn up the sacrifice that had been placed on the altar.

Resource Preparation:

- Prepare 12 bags for each team by filling small plastic trashcan liners with wadded up newspaper.
- Secure the tops of the plastic bags by tying a knot in them.

Resource Fun:

- Mark an altar area for each team with rope or masking tape.
- In this relay, each team will build an altar using their bags.
- When the leader signals, one person from each team will carry a bag to the area where their altar is to be built.
- He will return to his team and tag the next person who will carry the next bag to build the altar.
- The object is to get all 12 of the team bags to the altar area and in a pile to make the altar.

This game can be played with any lesson that has an altar as a main part of the story, such as when the Israelites came to the end of their journey and Joshua built an altar.

Variation:

- Form two teams that will pass one bag at a time down the line, from player to player, to build the altar.

Twister™ with a Twist

BIBLE STORY QUESTIONS

"Junk" Needed:
Small Post-It™ notes
Twister™ game

Kids love to play Twister™ and this game always seems to be tucked away in everyone's game closet. So bring it out for this fun learning game that can be used with any Bible story you're studying.
It's Twister™ with a twist!

Resource Preparation:

- Prepare a set of questions about the story being taught.
- Before beginning the traditional game, place a small Post-It™ note next to six of the possible spins.

Resource Fun:

- Four children can play at a time, or put out several Twister™ mats and accommodate all the children at once. It really is a lot of fun when everyone's playing at the same time.
- Spin the spinner to indicate where the children should place their foot or hand.
- Everyone moves on every spin. (If it lands on a right foot, red, then each child places his or her right foot on a red spot.)
- If the spin has a Post-It™ note next to it, before the children can move, someone must answer the question about the story.
- If no one can answer the question, the game is over and four new children are chosen to occupy the mat.
- After a question has been answered correctly, move the Post-It™ note to a new location.

Flick the Can
RAHAB & THE SPIES

"Junk" Needed:

A big supply of empty vegetable cans (or soda cans)

One piece of red yarn

Spoon

The Main Thing – Joshua 1—2

Rahab protected the spies when they came into Jericho. Knowing that the Israelites were going to invade Jericho, Rahab asked the spies if they would protect her in return. The spies told her to hang a red rope out her window to mark her home and she would not be harmed.

Resource Preparation:

- Mark one of the vegetable cans with a piece of red yarn.
- Build a wall with the cans, putting the one marked with the yarn in the midst of them.

Resource Fun:

- The children will take turns removing one can at a time from the wall by flicking the can with the spoon.
- Remove as many cans as possible without making the marked can (Rahab's home) fall.
- Once the children have gotten as far as they can, rearrange the cans and try again.

Storing Up Treasures
THE RICH MAN & HIS TREASURE

"Junk" Needed:

Large spoon for each child

Red construction paper

Supply of sand

Vegetable cans for each child

The Main Thing – Luke 12:13-21

The rich man was putting grain into his barn because he was always afraid he wouldn't have enough. When one barn was full, he would build another barn. His grain was like money. Some people today never want to give anything away or help anyone who needs their help because they are too busy keeping everything for themselves. God doesn't want us to be like that.

Resource Fun:

- Cut out a simple red barn from construction paper and glue it to the can.
- Place a can for each child about 20 feet away from the sand supply.
- The game begins with the child standing next to his or her can, with a large spoon in hand.
- When the leader says, "Fill the barn!" the children run to the sand, fill their spoon, and return to their barn/can to deposit the sand.
- Players will keep returning to the sand for another spoonful until their barn is full.

Gone Fishing
WAGON GAME

"Junk" Needed:

Butterfly net

Child's wagon

Poster board fish cutouts

Resource Preparation:

- Children have an opportunity to mimic being a fisherman catching fish from their boat. Any Bible stories that include fishing as a main element can incorporate this activity.
- Cut out 20 poster board fish that are about 5" in length.
- On 12 of the fish write questions about the story that is being taught. The other eight will be left blank.

Resource Fun:

- Scatter the poster board fish in the grass so they are not too close to one another.
- One child will get in the wagon and hold the butterfly net, while another child or leader pulls the wagon past the fish.
- The child in the wagon will try to catch one of the fish in his or her net as he goes past it and bring it back to the group.
- Once the wagon has returned to the starting point and the child has a fish, check the fish to see if it has a question on it. That question will be asked of the group.
- Give the child who caught the fish the first opportunity to answer the question.

All Washed Up
OUTSIDE GAME

"Junk" Needed:
Empty water bottles
Large squirt gun

This is definitely an outside activity!

Resource Preparation:

- Prepare a set of questions about the story being taught.
- Place 10 empty water bottles on an old table or on top of a fence, about 8" apart.

Resource Fun:

- Determine a stand-behind line depending on the power of the squirt gun being used.
- The kids will take turns trying to squirt one of the water bottles off its perch using the squirt gun.
- Time the kids so they squirt no longer than 20 seconds.
- Squirting stops when time is up or one of the bottles is knocked over.
- If the bottle goes over, then ask that child one of the questions that has been prepared.
- If she answers correctly, the bottle is removed permanently from play.
- If she answers incorrectly, place the bottle back in its position in the bottle line-up.
- Continue until all the bottles have been knocked down.

Water Bottles
RHYTHM SHAKERS

"Junk" Needed:
Craft paint (optional)
Empty water bottles
Rice

Resource Preparation & Fun:

It is optional, but adding color to the water bottles makes them even more appealing to the kids, and adds something extra.

- Water down some bright-colored craft paint (2-parts paint, 1-part water).
- Pour the paint into the water bottle and swirl it around the bottle until it is completely covered.
- Turn upside down and drain the extra paint out. Let it set overnight for the paint to dry.
- Once the paint is dry, add 1/3 cup of rice and replace the cap securely.
- Bring out these shakers to use as the children sing praise songs. What a neat way to liven up their praise!

Sequencing Boards
PUT THE STORY IN ORDER

The angel appeared to Mary to tell her ʼt she would have a baby.

"Junk" Needed:

2" x 4" board
Index cards

Resource Preparation:

Cut a 2" x 4" scrap of wood into a 10" length. Then cut slits across the wide side of the wood about 1" apart so an index card will stand upright in the slit.

Resource Fun:

- Write a paraphrase of the story on 6-9 index cards, one sentence on each card.
- Shuffle the cards.
- This activity can be done by the entire group, pairs of children, or individually.
- Give the child a set of story cards and the wooden sequencing board.
- The children will work at putting the cards in order as the story happened by sticking cards in the slots.
- The cards can easily be moved to a different slot if the child realizes a card was left out.

Mini-Bonus Ideas

Berry Boxes

- Dip the bottom of a plastic berry box in some bubble solution. As the box is moved through the air, it will make hundreds of little bubbles.

Blue Jeans

- Make pillows for a reading center by cutting the legs off a pair of blue jeans. Stuff the legs and sew the open edges together.
- Cut the legs off a pair of blue jeans, and sew the leg openings shut. Add a strap made from the leg material and some Velcro™ to the waist opening to close. Use the bag to carry supplies from home or to keep smaller loose items from becoming scattered in the classroom.

Carpet scraps

- Cut a small piece from a carpet scrap to use as an eraser for a dry erase board.

Hula Hoop

- Create a personal area for children to look up Bible verses or pray by laying down Hula Hoops. Their space has been defined and they like sitting in the middle of it.

Men's shirts

- Use large men's shirts for cover shirts when kids are involved in something messy. Cut the sleeves off at the elbow. Put them on the kids backwards so the buttons are going down the back. You only need to fasten the top button. It's quick, it's easy and it covers well.

Old sheets

- Rip old sheets into long strips and use them to tie legs together for a 3-legged race.
- Use long strips of sheeting for blindfolds by wrapping them around the child's head twice. Gets rid of being able to see through or peak around.
- Wrap someone in the long strips to portray Lazarus.

Scrabble® Tiles

- Mix several games of Scrabble® tiles together. Give each child one of the letter trays. Ask a question about the story, and the children race to see how fast they can spell the answer using the Scrabble® tiles.

Styrofoam™ egg cartons

- Clean the carton with soapy water and rinse thoroughly. Freeze water for ice cubes or chill Jell-O™ in the egg compartments.

Broom:

Sweep the brooms back and forth for a swishing sound.

Clothespins:

Attach a large jingle bell to the head of a clothespin (not the spring kind) using a piece of chenille stick. The smaller jingle bells don't make a significant sound, so get the largest one available.

Coconut:

Tap a coconut with a piece of dowel rod.

Film Canisters:

Put a tablespoon of dried beans in a film canister to make a shaker.

Paint Bucket Grid:

Drag a wooden spoon across the grid. It gives the effect of a washboard.

Paint Stir Sticks:

Attach both ends of sparkly material, about 18" long, to the end of a paint stir stick to make a loop. Wrap the ends with packing tape to secure the material to the stick. The children can wave these above their heads to the rhythm of their praise song.

Plastic or Metal Coffee Cans:

Put the plastic lids on them and tap on them with a pencil to use as a drum.

Styrofoam™ cups:

Turn the cups upside down and hit them against the floor to the rhythm.

Toilet Plunger:

Sit cross-legged with the plunger standing in front of you. Lift and hit it against the floor to the beat.

Wood dowels:

Cut 12" lengths of wood doweling to make rhythm sticks that can be struck against one another. Sand the ends so there's no danger of splinters.

Using Story Reinforcement Activities

Story Reinforcement Activities have become a valuable tool in children's ministry. These simple games can be used to test the children's comprehension of the story you are learning about or to review a previous lesson. The reason these games are such a valuable tool is that it is difficult to teach life lessons and applications to a child if they did not comprehend what actually took place in the story that was just told. It's a matter of moving from a very basic level to a higher thinking level. Sometimes we want to move on to that higher level of thinking, and it is possible, but the concept won't be learned based on its relationship to the Bible story. One of our objectives is to relate how God wants us to live to the examples He provides us in biblical accounts.

Story Reinforcement Activities quite often require that a set of questions be prepared that will require recalling information from the story. It may vary, but twelve questions are usually a good base to work with. Focus on writing questions that CANNOT be answered with "yes" or "no." Think about who, what, when, where, and how questions that could be answered about the story. Also, throw in a couple of questions that ask the children to think about how a certain person in the biblical account may have felt in the situation. (How do you think Peter felt when he got back in the boat after Jesus saved him?) This is where the child will start moving into a higher level of thinking. There are a few sets of questions included at the end of this article as examples of the kinds of questions to prepare for these games.

In most cases, the **Story Reinforcement Activities** are set up so that the children do something that they consider play. As a result of successfully accomplishing the play task, they don't get rewarded with a prize, but rather they earn the right to answer a question about the story. If the children are not able to answer the question, instead of making them feel defeated or embarrassed, empower them by giving them permission to choose someone from their group to assist them. This really helps with children who are new to church and learning the Bible, because they can easily feel alienated by those who have much more knowledge.

Before the story is presented, prepare the children by telling them that they will be playing a game that will require them to remember what the story is about. As you begin to use **Story Reinforcement Activities**, the children will learn that they are more successful in the game later on when they listen intently now. The result is a big positive in that the kids pay closer attention as the story is being presented.

Questions for Story: Jesus Walks on the Water

1. What were the disciples going to do after a long day with the people? (They were going fishing.)

2. What was Jesus going to do while the disciples were fishing? (Go up the mountain to pray.)

3. How did the weather change when the sun went down? (A terrible storm blew up.)

4. What did Jesus remember when He saw the storm coming up? (He remembered how frightened the disciples had been at another time when they were on the boat during a storm.)

5. How did Jesus get from the shore to the boat that the disciples were in? (He walked on the water.)

6. What did the disciples think they saw out on the water? (A ghost)

7. Which disciple yelled out to Jesus, "If it is You, Lord, tell me to come to You walking on the water"? (Peter)

8. What did Peter do when Jesus said, "Come"? (He jumped over the side of the boat and started walking to Jesus.)

9. Why do you think Peter got scared all of a sudden? (He took his eyes off Jesus and saw what a dangerous thing he was doing.)

10. What happened to Peter when he looked around at the waves? (He began to sink.)

11. What did Jesus do when Peter cried out for help? (Jesus reached out and grabbed Peter's hand.)

12. What did the disciples do when Jesus and Peter climbed back in the boat? (They worshiped Jesus.)

13. If you were on the boat, what do you think you would've done when you saw Jesus walking on the water?

Questions for Story: Jonah

1. What did God want Jonah to do that Jonah didn't want to do? (Go tell some people he didn't like about God.)

2. What did Jonah decide to do instead of doing what God told him to do? (He decided to get on a ship and head the other direction.)

3. What happened while Jonah was asleep down in the bottom of the ship? (A big storm came up.)

4. How did the crew of the ship lighten the load during the storm? (They threw cargo overboard.)

5. What did the captain of the ship want Jonah to do for them? (The captain wanted Jonah to pray to God to save them.)

6. The crew decided someone on the ship was causing God to be mad. Who did they decide it was? (Jonah)

7. What did Jonah tell the crew to do to him? (Jonah told the men to throw him overboard.)

8. What happened to the sea when they threw Jonah into the water? (It calmed down.)

9. What happened to Jonah when he was thrown in the sea? (A big fish swallowed him.)

10. What do you think Jonah thought about while he was in the belly of the fish?

11. How long did Jonah stay inside the big fish? (3 days and 3 nights)

12. What did the fish do with Jonah after Jonah prayed to God? (It spit Jonah up on the shore.)

13. What do you think Jonah did as soon as the fish spit him out?

14. What did Jonah do after his experience with disobeying God and the big fish? (Jonah decided to go where God told him to go.)

Questions for Story: Paul Is Shipwrecked

1. Why was Paul a prisoner? (He spoke up for God.)

2. Why was Paul on the ship? (He was being taken to a different place for his trial.)

3. When the storm was blowing up, Paul told the crew, "Even though the ship will be lost, no one will lose" what? (No one will lose his life.)

4. How do you think the men felt about Paul being on the ship?

5. What happened to the boat Paul was on when the storm blew up? (The boat fell apart.)

6. What did the people on the island do for the men who floated up to shore? (The people on the island built a fire for the shipwrecked men.)

7. What came out of the fire? (A snake.)

8. What did the snake do to Paul? (The snake bit Paul.)

9. What do you think Paul thought when the snake bit him?

10. Why did the people on the island watch Paul when he was bit? (They thought the snake bite would kill him.)

11. What did the islanders think when Paul didn't fall over dead from the snake bite? (They thought Paul was a god.)

12. What did the ruler of the island want Paul to do for him? (The ruler wanted Paul to heal his father.)

13. What happened when Paul prayed for the ruler of the island's father? (The father was healed.)

14. What did Paul get a chance to do because of the miracle? (He got a chance to talk about Jesus.)

Using Masking Tape

The off-white masking tape is fine for most of these activities. But if you want to add a little pizzazz with some fun colors, order a pack of multi-color masking tape from Oriental Trading (www.orientaltrading.com). This color pack will cost less per roll than the off-white purchased in a discount store, but has to be purchased in a variety 10-pack.

I've not found a surface that I am apprehensive about using masking tape on. The main thing you need to remember is to remove the masking tape in a reasonable amount of time. It will pull up easily from carpeting or off of windows for about three weeks.

Index

Bible Story

Old Testament

New Testament

Bible Verse

Genesis

Bible Verse Continued

Games

Resources

Resources Continued

Resources Continued

Resources Continued

Themes

My Junk Notes

My Junk Notes